0–8054–2091–6

Published by Broadman & Holman Publishers, Nashville, Tennessee
Editorial Team: Leonard G. Goss, John Landers
Cover & Interior Design: Identity Design Inc., Dallas, Texas

Dewey Decimal Classification: 242.2
Subject Heading: DEVOTIONAL EXERCISES

Every Day Light™
CWR, Waverley Abbey House, Waverley Lane, Farnham, Surrey GU9 8EP

EDL Classic, *Born to Praise* Text 1998 © Selwyn Hughes
Material taken from *Every Day with Jesus* The Purpose and Power of Praise 1982
Revised edition in this format 1998 © Selwyn Hughes

AUSTRALIA: CMC Australasia
P.O. Box 519, Belmont, Victoria 3216 Tel: (03) 5241 3288

CANADA: CMC Distribution Ltd.
P.O. Box 7000, Niagara on the Lake, Ontario L0S 1J0 Tel: 1 800 325 1297

INDIA: Full Gospel Literature Stores
254 Kilpauk Garden Road, Chennai 600010 Tel: (44) 644 3073

KENYA: Keswick Bookshop
P.O. Box 10242, Nairobi Tel: (02) 331692/226047

MALAYSIA: Salvation Book Centre (M)
23 Jalan SS2/64, Sea Park, 47300 Petaling Jaya, Selangor Tel: (3) 7766411

NEW ZEALAND: CMC New Zealand Ltd.
P.O. Box 949, 205 King Street South, Hastings
Tel: (6) 8784408, Toll free: 0800 333639

NIGERIA: FBFM, (Every Day with Jesus)
Prince's Court, 37 Ahmed Onibudo Street, P.O. Box 70952, Victoria Island
Tel: 01 2617721, 616832, 4700218

REPUBLIC OF IRELAND: Scripture Union
40 Talbot Street, Dublin 1 Tel: (01) 8363764

SINGAPORE: Campus Crusade Asia Ltd.
315 Outram Road, 06–08 Tan Boon Liat Building, Singapore 169074
Tel: (65) 222 3640

SOUTH AFRICA: Struik Christian Books (Pty Ltd)
P.O. Box 193, Maitland 7405, Cape Town Tel: (021) 551 5900

SRI LANKA: Christombu Investments
27 Hospital Street, Colombo 1 Tel: (1) 433142/328909

USA: CMC Distribution
P.O. Box 644, Lewiston, New York 14092–0644 Tel: 1 800 325 1297

QUIET TIME

Daily
You pour Your blessings
on us, Lord
yet we turn to the
ash-heap of yesterday
pawing through the ruins
searching for You.
Help us to remember that
YOU don't live in
yesterday
any more than WE do!
Teach us to receive all Your
now blessings
even when they're
cleverly disguised as
unsolvable problems.

© Susan Lenzkes

Signature Series
SELWYN HUGHES

BORN

TO PRAISE

Every Day Light for
Your Journey

BROADMAN
& HOLMAN
PUBLISHERS

NASHVILLE, TENNESSEE

GRATITUDE TO GOD

To worship God must be
the consuming passion of
the heart, whether we express
it in old ways or new ways,
in silence or with shouts,
in stillness or with dancing.

— Graham Kendrick

CREATED
TO PRAISE

For Reading and Meditation: Psalm 107:1–22

"Oh that men would praise the LORD
for his goodness" (v. 8 KJV).

Today we begin studying the thrilling theme of praise.
We shall also bring alongside the thought of thanksgiving, as
it is a close relative of praise. The two have been referred to as
the "Siamese twins of the Christian family."

Although the thoughts contained in the two words are
quite distinct and separate—we praise God for who He is;
we thank Him for what He does—we must not hold to these
distinctions too rigidly, as they sometimes merge into each other.

Why Were We Created?

We begin our studies by asking ourselves an important
question: Why were we created? The best answer to that
question is contained in the words of the Westminster
Catechism: "Man's chief end is to glorify God and enjoy Him
forever." In other words, we were created to praise. In the light
of this, how many of our waking hours are given to the praise

of God? Isn't it true to say that we spend more time worrying, grumbling, and complaining than we do in praise of our Creator? Yet when we pause to thank God, what endless reasons can we find to be grateful!

Someone has said that there are two types of Christians in the world: those who take for granted and those who take with gratitude. Which are you? A Christian who knows how to fill his life with praise faces life buoyantly and confidently because in every situation, no matter how dark and difficult, he is conscious of God's mercy streaming in from heaven. So make up your mind on this first day of our excursion into the subject of praise to become a praising and thankful Christian. Learn to praise the Lord at all times—up times, down times, dark times, bright times—and I promise you that life will soon take on a new and different meaning.

O God, forgive me for the blessings I take
for granted rather than with gratitude. Teach me
over these next few weeks the art of praising
You at all times. For Jesus' sake. Amen.

"Man's chief end is to glorify God and enjoy Him forever."

A T   A L L   T I M E S ?

For Reading and Meditation: Psalm 34:1–22

"I will extol the LORD at all times; his praise will always be on my lips" (v. 1).

We ended yesterday by saying that one of our greatest needs as Christians is learning to be a praising and thankful people, and not to take things for granted, but with gratitude.

Created to Praise

The Bible fairly bulges with the truth that we are created to praise, and encourages us to praise our Creator energetically, vociferously, and at every opportunity. We are told by both Old and New Testament writers that it is our duty to praise the Lord, and there are times when the Almighty Himself takes up the issue, not merely to encourage our praise but to demand it (Ps. 50:13–17, 22–23).

There can be no doubt to even the most casual reader of the Scriptures that praise is as important a spiritual focus as prayer, and that without it our lives become jaded and impoverished. In our text today, the psalmist tells us that he praised God "at all times." Can we really be expected to praise God on all occasions and at every opportunity? Surely it means most or many or almost all times. One can't be expected to be full of praise when the days are dark and gray, or the doctor is calling every day, looking graver each time he leaves. Not so: "I will extol the Lord at all times," says the psalmist. "His praise will always be on my lips."

Take a leaf out of the psalmist's book and follow his advice. Make this day a day of continued praise. Magnify the Lord in your heart in a special way. Reflect on the wonder of the fact that you, a soiled sinner, can come into His presence and linger there—as long as you like. Rejoice in the fact that He belongs to you and you belong to Him, and nothing can separate you from His love.

O Father, this day I want to be filled
with unceasing praise—praise such as I have
never given and never known before.
For Jesus' sake I ask it. Amen.

Praise is as important a spiritual focus as prayer.

BURSTING THE DRUM

For Reading and Meditation: Isaiah 43:1–21

"This people have I formed for myself; they shall show forth my praise" (v. 21 KJV).

We continue meditating on the importance and necessity of praise. I can never understand how it is that over the centuries the Christian religion has become associated with gloom. Even in Old Testament times, as we can see from our text today, God encouraged His people to exhibit a life of praise. Praise, to the Old Testament saints, was vocal and vociferous.

Vocal Praise

The early church was so joyful on the day of Pentecost that they were accused of being drunk. Modern Christians do not come under this dark suspicion! The first Franciscans had to be reproved for laughing in church because they were so radiantly happy. The early Methodists took some of their tunes from operas and set their songs to dance music. General Booth told the first Salvationists that if they felt the Spirit moving them during a hymn or prayer, they could jump. They did!

Dr. Farmer, a brilliant organist and musician, once adjudicated at a music festival where a Salvation Army band was playing. He appealed to the drummer, a fairly new convert, not to hit the drum so hard, to which the man replied, "I'm so happy, sir, I could burst the blessed drum." He turned to another new convert who was playing French horn and asked him also to restrain himself. "But sir," said the horn player, "I'm so full of joy, I want to blow this thing straight!"

It's easy to hear stories such as these and think ourselves a little superior. We might even think, "Well, that was another generation. Today's religion is more sophisticated." The faith of Jesus and exuberance are not something to be set apart. They belong together and must be brought together—here in the twentieth century.

O God, make us once again a people of praise. Help us to be exuberant, joyful, infectiously happy, so that cold conventionalities thaw in our presence. For Jesus' sake. Amen.

The faith of Jesus and exuberance are not something to be set apart.

WHAT'S HAPPENED
TO US?

For Reading and Meditation: Psalm 100:1–5

"Enter his gates with thanksgiving and his
courts with praise" (v. 4).

We saw yesterday that the early Methodists and Salvationists manifested a joy and exuberance that in some sections of today's church would be greatly frowned upon. W. E. Sangster wrote, "It is when the fires in the individual heart die down that convention frowns on exuberance and an air of superiority is affected toward those who cannot restrain their joyous praise."

Church history is full of instances showing that when a movement of the Spirit begins, those involved in it demonstrate an unrestrained delight that later gives way to formalism and convention. Allowing for the fact that new movements and new beginnings excite a good deal of natural enthusiasm, I cannot believe it is God's purpose for His people to lapse into dull conventionalism and empty routine. May I, through these pages, make a plea for a livelier and more enthusiastic approach to worship and praise in our churches. Our services ought to be centers of glowing gratitude where the saints, intoxicated with the wonder of their salvation, praise and magnify the Savior together.

Of course, there will be those like David's wife Michal (2 Sam. 6:16) who will abhor any semblance of joy, and will murmur something about fanaticism and emotionalism. But there is nothing more beautiful and wonderful than to be in the midst of God's people when their hearts are bursting with praise. A Christian has only to look at Jesus to want to praise Him. A glimpse of Him sets all the bells ringing in one's heart. Charles Wesley spoke for us all when he wrote:

> In the heavenly Lamb
>   Thrice happy I am,
> And my heart it doth dance at the
>   sound of His Name.

O God, forgive us that we are so often thought by the world to be sober and dignified when it is a travesty of our true traditions.

DOES GOD NEED OUR PRAISE?

For Reading and Meditation: Ephesians 5:5–21

"Always giving thanks to God the Father for everything" (v. 20).

Having examined together the importance and necessity of praise, we turn now to consider a question which is often raised whenever the subject of praise is discussed: Why does God insist on being praised? Is it because He needs constant reassurance that He is good and great? Or is it because there is a need in God that only praise can fill?

Problems with Praise

This question troubled me greatly when I first became a Christian. I was told by my pastor and elders, "Now that you are a Christian you must read your Bible every day, pray as often as you can, and praise the Lord at all times." I got on fairly well with my daily Bible reading and prayer, but when it came to praise, I encountered serious difficulties. I kept thinking to myself, *Is God so insecure that He wants me to boost His ego by my praise?* The idea that God craved praise, like a vain woman angling for compliments, was abhorrent to me. Then someone gave me a book in which the author pointed out that while God does not need our praise ("it is not in our power to add to His plenitude"), He delights in it nevertheless. The author told the story of a Sunday school teacher who received a cheap penknife as a present from one of his students. It was the product of hoarded pennies. Did he need it? No! Did he want it? Yes!

God does not need our gifts. He does not need our thanks. But does He want them? Oh yes! In the narrow sense of the word, nothing we do can meet a need in God, for He has no needs. He is, however, a Father who desires the gratitude of His children and delights in their thanks, no matter how hesitant or inadequate they may be.

O Father, although I know I cannot meet a need in You, for You have no needs, yet I see that I can bring joy and delight to Your heart through my praise. Help me to give it, not grudgingly or sparingly, but freely, joyously and perpetually. Amen.

God is a Father who desires the gratitude of His children and delights in their thanks.

PRAISE DOES US GOOD

For Reading and Meditation: James 5:10–20

"Those who have reason to be thankful should continually be singing praises to the Lord" (v. 13 TLB).

We saw yesterday that whatever reasons God has for insisting on our praise, it is not because it meets a need in Him—for God has no needs. If there is one truth beyond dispute among Christians, it is the perfection of God. He is uncreated, self-sufficient, and lacks nothing. He therefore does not need our gifts, sacrifices, or even our praise.

If God doesn't need our thanks, then why does He so often encourage us, through His Word, to be thankful? The answer is simple though it must not be considered simplistic: we need it. It does us good to be thankful. In one sense, being thankful does more for us than it does for God, although, of course, we must not forget that He finds great pleasure in it also.

Modern-day Psychology

Modern-day psychology is discovering something in this century that has been a law of life ever since man appeared on earth, namely, that we are not made happy by what we acquire but by what we appreciate. In other words, the degree to which we are thankful or appreciative determines our happiness in every area of life. When we acquire something new, be it a new house, a new car, or new clothes, we are usually keenly appreciative. However, six months later, the same object (now no longer so deeply appreciated) brings us not one-tenth of the excitement and pleasure it brought us originally.

A Spirit of Thankfulness

Our thankfulness and appreciation diminish, and when that happens, boredom sets in. And not only boredom, other, much more serious, consequences occur when we lose the spirit of thankfulness and praise.

O God, teach me the art of continual thankfulness, and help me never to become bored with You, for I know that if that happens, then life will soon disintegrate. Help me, Lord Jesus. Amen.

Being thankful does more for us than it does for God.

A WRONG FOCUS

For Reading and Meditation: 1 Thessalonians 5:14–23

"Give thanks in all circumstances,
for this is God's will" (v. 18).

Someone has said that a neurotic is a person who focuses more on what he lacks than on what he possesses. Many of us live on the borders of neurosis because we fail to recognize the blessings of God in our lives and the way in which He is working all things out for good.

Someone wrote to me, "For weeks I had been going about concentrating on the difficulties in my life, and I had become deeply depressed. Then something you said in *Every Day with Jesus* caused me to look at the good things that were happening to me, and instantly the depression lifted."

This letter doesn't surprise me, for I have come to see that life works like this: If we focus on our difficulties, we get depressed; if we focus on God's mercies, we will be uplifted. It's so easy to concentrate on the negative things in our lives. So many of our waking hours are spent thinking about what is going wrong—business problems, disagreements, broken possessions—that we use up emotional energy which could be put to better use. Some people complain because God put thorns on roses; others thank Him for putting roses on thorns. How much time do we focus on what is going right—usually the 80 percent taken for granted areas?

Express Gratitude

A great thinker once said, "Man is not made happy by what he has but by what he is thankful for." Whether it be material possessions, success, friendship, or love, every factor which might bring us greater happiness only makes us actually happier as we appreciate it. It's so simple. Someone gives you a gift, and as you thank them for it, they are gratified. Thankfulness rewards the giver, but it rewards the receiver too. To receive without being thankful is to miss the joy of appreciation which is the real gift. A gift unappreciated is, in one sense, ungiven.

Father God, I know You are trying
to teach me that I am fulfilled not by what
I possess but by what I am thankful for.
Burn this truth deeper and deeper into
my spirit. For Jesus' sake. Amen.

If we focus on God's mercies, we will be uplifted.

As we
praise and worship,
God steps out of
his mystery into
our history and we
move from our history
into his mystery.

— Source unknown

WEEK 2

MADE
FOR PRAISE

All too often our faith is
earth-bound and we find it hard
to believe that God can do
anything that our minds cannot
explain. It is only as we spend
time worshipping God,
concentrating on the nature of
his Person — especially his
greatness and love — that
our faith begins to rise.

— David Watson

EXPRESSION DEEPENS IMPRESSION

For Reading and Meditation: Psalm 107:1–43

"Has the Lord redeemed you? Then speak out! Tell others he has saved you" (v. 2 TLB).

We continue meditating on the fact that we are made in the inner structure of our being for praise, and it is only when we praise that we complete ourselves and experience fulfillment. We saw the other day that we cannot really enjoy anything until we express in some way our appreciation of that enjoyment. C. S. Lewis said, "We delight to praise the things we enjoy because the praise not merely expresses the pleasure we feel but completes it." Praise consummates the experience.

A Law of Life

Why does a young man in love enjoy telling his fiancée how beautiful and adorable she is? Is it because he read somewhere in a book a chapter on the importance of giving compliments? No. It is because he instinctively feels that the delight he experiences can only be fully felt when it is expressed. It is a law of life that expression deepens impression.

Have you ever found yourself sharing your feelings with someone about a pleasant experience you had, only to find that as you share it, you feel a warm inner glow that surpasses even the joy you knew in the experience itself? That was the law of "expression/impression" at work.

W. E. Sangster, in one of his Westminster Sermons, said, "One of the worst moments for an atheist is when he feels thankful and has no One to thank." How sad to watch a glorious sunset but to have to keep silent about it because the people you are with are more interested in the flames of a garden bonfire. How much more sad, however, to meditate on the goodness and greatness of God and fail to appreciate it because no expression is given to the joy and delight felt.

My God and Father, how can I ever thank You enough for designing me in this wonderful way. The more praise I express, the more I have to express. And the cycle will never end. Praise Your wonderful Name. Amen.

"Praise not merely expresses the pleasure we feel but completes it."

AND THAT
IS HEAVEN

For Reading and Meditation: Revelation 4:1–11

"Day and night they never stop saying:
'Holy, holy, holy is the Lord'" (v. 8).

Yesterday we touched on the fact that it is only as we express things that we really experience them, for there is a law in life that says expression deepens impression. This is so even when our expressions are weak and inadequate.

Delight in the Creator

What if we could praise to perfection, utterly "get out" the appreciation that wells up inside us? What then? Well, the object would be fully appreciated and, in return, our joy would reach its fullest consummation. If it were possible for a human being to love, enjoy, and delight in the Creator to the fullest extent possible, and give expression to that feeling in a continued and uninterrupted form, then that person would be in the most perfect bliss imaginable. It would be heaven! Until I understood this, I thought that heaven, described in the text before us today as a place of unceasing praise, would be rather dull and boring.

I pictured it, I am afraid, as an interminable church service, but I failed to see that our praise here on earth is as nothing compared to how we shall praise our Creator when we get to heaven.

Imagine being in a state where you are in perfect love with God, satiated with Him, drunk with Him, overwhelmed by a delight which, far from being pent-up within you, flows out in free and unrestrained expression. Imagine, too, what it would be like to express the praise you feel freely, without restriction or inhibition. In the giving and expressing of such praise, a human being would experience such delight, such overwhelming joy, that it would fill his personality to its utmost limits. And that is heaven!

O Father, all I can say is this,
"If here it is so blessed, what must it be up there!"
I can't wait to meet You and to praise
You with unrestricted joy. Amen.

Imagine what it would be like to express freely the praise you feel.

Not A Demand—
An Offer

For Reading and Meditation: Matthew 16:21–28

"Whoever loses his life for me will find it" (v. 25).

Over the past few days we have been coming to grips with an important question: "Why does God insist that we praise Him?" We have seen that apart from the joy our praises bring to the heart of God, praise also meets a deep need in us. However, there is another vital reason God invites us to praise Him. Through the process of praise, God is able to communicate His presence more fully to us. As we give ourselves to Him in praise, He, in turn, is able to give Himself to us. Why should this be?

Self-giving is one of the established principles in the universe "Give, and it will be given to you," said Jesus (Luke 6:38). Is this a principle which holds good only for men and women? No. God is bound by it too.

Giving All the Way

The Almighty will never ask us to do something He hasn't done Himself. He moved toward us through the door of the incarnation where He gave Himself to us, and then later, at the point of crucifixion, He gave Himself for us. It was giving all the way. By going through the door of self-giving and abiding by His own eternal principles, God has demonstrated the truth that in order to receive one must first give. He gave Himself to us (and for us) and, as a result, millions have responded to His love by going through the door of self-giving and giving themselves to Him. It is as if God is saying, "Nothing of value can be received in this universe without self-giving. As you go through the door of self-giving and focus upon Me in adoration and praise, so I am able to move through that same door and affirm My presence in your hearts." Seen in this light, His insistence on being praised is not so much a demand as an offer.

O God, now it all makes sense! You insist on my praise because as I give to You so You are able to give to me. It is my interests You have at heart— not Your own. I am eternally grateful. Amen.

Through the incarnation He gave Himself to us; through the crucifixion, He gave Himself for us.

THE ROOT OF SIN

For Reading and Meditation: Daniel 5:13–31

"The God in whose hand is your breath,
and whose are all your ways, you have not
honored" (v. 23 RSV).

While we must not lose sight of the fact that the prime purpose of praise is to honor and glorify God, what praise does for us is so important that we must continue discussing it.

The Temptation of Eve

There is a good case for arguing that the root of sin is thanklessness. The temptation of Eve involved getting her to doubt whether God should be thanked—or blamed. The serpent persuaded Eve to overlook the fact that God had given her everything she needed, and to concern herself with the one thing she was denied—the fruit of the tree of knowledge of good and evil. Look how cunningly the serpent approached her: "God knows that when you eat of it your eyes will be opened, and you will be like God" (Gen. 3:5 RSV). Eve then decided to focus on the thing she was denied rather than thank God for all that He had provided.

It is basically the same decision, by the way, which contributes to lack of mental health in those whom our society describes as neurotic. The neurotic is a person who is usually obsessed by what he feels he lacks, and focuses on that more than on the things he has. He focuses on negative rather than on positive factors.

In the text before us today, God reprimands Belshazzar for failing to recognize that He was the source of his existence. The apostle Paul told the Christians in Rome a similar truth when he said, "They are without excuse; for although they knew God they did not honor him as God or give thanks to him" (Rom. 1:20–21 RSV).

Thanklessness lies at the root of mankind's sin and most of our everyday sins as well!

> O God, save me I pray from the sin of thanklessness. Keep me awake and alert to all the positive things that are going on in my life—and help me to be continually thankful. For Jesus' sake. Amen.

Thanklessness lies at the root of mankind's sin.

HEAL THY PRAISE

For Reading and Meditation: Psalm 92:1–15

"It is good to give thanks to the LORD, to sing praises to thy name" (v. 1 RSV).

Have you ever considered how praise is essential not only to our relationship with God but in relationships with one another too? Thanklessness was a major factor in the destruction of Eve's relationship with God; it destroys human relationships as well. "Love makes the world go round," goes an old romantic song, but it is only half true. If it is love that starts our world going around, then, believe me, it is thankfulness that keeps it spinning.

Thankfulness Expressed

The most exciting romance or, for that matter, marriage will eventually grind to a halt if there is no day-to-day thankfulness expressed in a smile, a kiss, or a word of appreciation. C. S. Lewis said, "The people who praise most are those who enjoy life most." He went on to say, "I had not noticed how the humblest and at the same time the most balanced and capacious minds praised most, while the cranks, misfits and malcontents praised least." Isn't it true that the best critics are those who find something to praise in even the most imperfect book while the bad critic would have us read only that which accords with his own high and often impossible standards?

Dyspeptics

A doctor once told me that the happiest and healthiest people are those who are quick to praise—not the flatterers or the insincere, but those who look for and who are quick to recognize the praiseworthy aspects of every situation. Dyspeptics, I am told by those who work in the medical profession, are notorious grumblers. Is their dyspepsia due to their inner disharmony? Perhaps. One thing is sure, when we fail to praise that which is good and worthy of recognition, we are depleted, starved, and poisoned, and we lose our sense of well-being.

Father, something is being burned into my consciousness—the laws of life. I am not able to escape them. Nor would I, for to escape them would be foolishness to the highest degree. I would accept them and be what You designed me to be. Amen.

If it is love that starts our world going around, it is thankfulness that keeps it spinning.

I N N E R   D I V I S I O N

For Reading and Meditation: Colossians 3:1–15

"Let the peace of Christ rule in your hearts,
since . . . you were called to peace" (v. 15).

We said yesterday that the healthiest and happiest people are those who are quick and ready to praise. Someone has defined *praise* as "inner health made audible." What is the connection between a readiness to praise and inner and outer health? Well, quite simply it is this: we are made in our inmost beings for praise. God designed us to be praising beings, and if this is not our chief characteristic, the machinery of life gets out of gear—for we are geared to creation. And what is the purpose of our creation? We see it again in Revelation 4:11, "And for thy pleasure they are and were created" (KJV).

A Divided Being

Our first responsibility, of course, is to praise God, but we have a responsibility, too, to praise others. Some are vociferous in their praise of God but extremely grudging in their praise of others. Such a person will never be truly happy (or healthy) because he is a divided being.

A man I knew in a church I once pastored would shout the praises of God in every service, but at home he was a sour and surly individual. At the request of his family, I spoke to him about it, but he appeared blind to the problem. The law of life then took its toll. He became crippled with rheumatism, and within a year or two was a chronic invalid. His doctor said he was tied up with inner conflicts, and although not all rheumatism starts this way, it was so in his case, according to the doctor. He was a divided person, and as such he was working against the grain of life. He was a praising person in church but a surly and cantankerous person at home. And life recorded its verdict— chronic invalidism.

O God, help me to be a whole person—not a divided person. I want to be at one with You and others. For Your own dear Name's sake. Amen.

God designed us to be praising beings.

L O A D E D W I T H
B E N E F I T S

For Reading and Meditation: Psalm 68:1–19

"Blessed be the Lord, who daily loadeth us with benefits . . ." (v. 19 KJV).

Quietly we are coming to the conclusion that praise in relation to God is the right thing to do, and in relation to ourselves, it is the profitable thing to do. It is the right thing to do because to take benefits from God without a thought or a word of thanks is mean and contemptible. Even a dog wags its tail when given a bone. It is the profitable thing to do because when we praise and give thanks, we do what we were designed to do, and life rewards us with health and happiness.

When I use the word *profitable* here, I am not thinking cynically, like Robert Walpole, who said that "gratitude is a lively sense of future favours," nor of the agnostic who caricatured the psalmists as praising God for what they could get out of Him: "God, I know you like praise—do this for me and I'll give you some." I mean profitable in the sense we have been discussing—that a Christian who is quick to praise and swift to thank lives in a constant state of happiness and goodwill.

Barricade Against Depression

This approach to life builds a barricade against depression and contributes to good mental health. Being thankful for the good things that come to us rather than just grumbling about the bad things that go on around us helps us to keep our minds balanced and functioning in the way God designed them to do.

It is a fact of human life that mercies can be found at the heart of tragedies, and if we are alert we can see something to be grateful for in even the most dark and dismal circumstances. When we are unaware of God's love for us, it is often because we have not tried to perceive it. To see His love, you have only to look.

O Father, give me eyes to see Your goodness that
You shower upon me on every hand; and when
I see it, help me not merely to look at it, or even gaze
at it, but to stare at it—and give thanks. Amen.

A Christian who is quick to praise lives in a constant state of happiness.

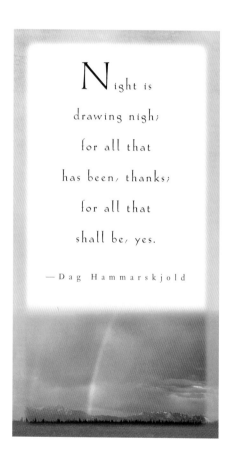

N ight is

drawing nigh;

for all that

has been, thanks;

for all that

shall be, yes.

— Dag Hammarskjold

DEFEAT TO VICTORY

Prayer is a silence and

a shouting burst of

praise a thanksgiving

welling up and out of us

in spite of everything.

— Kathy Keay

THE SACRIFICE OF PRAISE

For Reading and Meditation: Hebrews 13:5–21

"Let us offer the sacrifice of praise to God continually" (v. 15 KJV).

"God," said C. S. Lewis, "is a great Giver and a great Lover." There is nothing which delights Him more than having His gifts received and appreciated."

At times, however, we are not quick to recognize the gifts and blessings of God, and then our task is to exercise faith—to believe and to receive. Faith is an expression of the willingness to receive God's love—His gifts—and thankfulness is the emotional reaction to the exercise of faith.

Think it through a little further with me. On God's part there is the offer of love—free, unmerited favor. On our part there is the decision of faith—an active choice to believe in God's love toward us and receive it; and gratitude and thankfulness is the emotional response we have to that decision. On some occasions there has to be what someone described as "an adoring venture of faith," or else there would be no feeling of thankfulness.

When Cancer Strikes

When cancer strikes, for example, it isn't easy to be a praising person, though I am surprised at the number of times when talking to Christians who have succumbed to this dreadful disease how so many of them find reasons to be grateful. The ministry of praise at such times may be what the Bible terms "the sacrifice of praise"—thanksgiving that has blood upon it. There are Christians who are so in touch with God that they believe God's love surrounds them even when they are overtaken by a tragedy such as I have described. It strains faith and taxes it to its utmost limit, but saints down through the ages rise up to testify that it is possible. The sacrifice of such thanksgiving is, indeed, precious in God's sight.

O God, give me the kind of faith that trusts You even when it can't trace You, and survives even the most overwhelming tests. For Jesus' sake. Amen.

"God is a great Giver and a great Lover. There is nothing which delights Him more than having His gifts received and appreciated."

W   E   E   K   D A Y 2   T   H   R   E   E

VICTORY
THROUGH PRAISE

For Reading and Meditation: 2 Chronicles 20:1–24

"And when they began to sing and praise,
the LORD set an ambush against the men . . .
so that they were routed" (v. 22 RSV).

We shall now turn to examine some specific biblical situations where praise played a prominent part in turning defeat into victory. In a way that is impossible to define properly, praise releases God's power into difficult situations and sets the stage for great spiritual victories. We begin with the story of Jehoshaphat.

The Story of Jehoshaphat

The situation described in 2 Chronicles 20 was extremely critical. A vast army was invading the kingdom of King Jehoshaphat, who laid out his plight before the Lord in fear and trembling. Through his intercession, God showed him the secret of victory. He was to place in the forefront of his army a selected group of singers whose task it was to go ahead of the army, singing and praising the Lord. It sounds like a pretty far-fetched idea, doesn't it? Imagine a modern-day general ordering his troops to walk toward the enemy behind a small group of people who are singing praises to God! It is the kind of situation that causes human reason to balk. What happened to Jehoshaphat and his men? As the singers went out ahead of the army, God gave them such a victory that their enemies were routed, and peace came once again to the land. The secret of this story is found in verse 15: "The battle is not yours, but God's."

Many of us are constantly defeated by our circumstances because we are not ready to accept that the battle is God's—not ours. Even when we realize our own powerlessness to cope with the problem, we are afraid to let ourselves go and trust God's power. We may not understand how praise brings victory, but then we are not called to understand—we are called to stand.

Lord, in this conflict between acceptance and understanding, help me to put acceptance first. Help me to see that praise is a proven path to victory, and enable me to practice it—today. Amen.

Praise releases God's power into difficult situations.

THE FALL
OF JERICHO

For Reading and Meditation: Joshua 6:1–20

"All the people shall shout with a great shout;
and the wall of the city shall fall down flat"
(v. 5 KJV).

Today we look at another biblical account where praise released God's power into a situation and turned defeat into victory. The city of Jericho was a fortified stronghold. The Israelites, who had wandered for forty years in the wilderness, certainly didn't have the weapons needed to overthrow such a secure community. God told Joshua to march around Jericho six days in succession. On the seventh day he was to get the priests to blow their trumpets and shout.

The Example of Joshua

Joshua trusted God, but I wonder what you and I would have done if we had been in that procession? Would we have dismissed the idea as foolhardy and ridiculous? See what happened! "And suddenly the walls of Jericho crumbled and fell before them, and the people of Israel poured into the city from every side and captured it!" (v. 20 TLB). We don't know what the Israelites shouted, but I feel quite sure it was a shout of praise. The example of Joshua and the destruction of Jericho clearly demonstrate that God wins our victories by means and principles that look utterly foolish and contradictory to human wisdom and ingenuity.

In some of life's situations, God tells us to trust Him, praise Him, and watch Him work. All He requires from us is the step of faith on our part to do what He asks, whether we understand it or not. Are you at this moment confronted by walls of great difficulty that threaten and overwhelm you, and although you have prayed, you still cannot see the victory? Well, now try praise. This does not mean that prayer is unimportant; it is definitely an important pathway to God. But so is praise. So praise Him, trust Him, and watch Him work.

O Father, I praise You today from the bottom of my heart that You are the God of miracles and wonders. I believe that as I praise You, my "walls of Jericho" will come crashing down. Hallelujah!

God tells us to praise Him, trust Him, and watch Him work.

THE WAY OF DELIVERANCE

For Reading and Meditation: 2 Samuel 22:1–20

"I call to the LORD, who is worthy of praise,
and I am saved from my enemies" (v. 4).

We continue examining biblical situations in which praise proved most powerful. I wonder, am I speaking to someone today who is in a spiritual mess? Everything in your life seems to have gone wrong, and you drag yourself through one crisis only to face another. Day by day you are being pulled down into a vortex of despair that threatens to engulf your soul. Then lift up your head and throw back your shoulders because I believe this is going to be a day of deliverance for you.

God's Servant, David

Consider God's servant, David, in his struggles against the heathen armies of his day. Beset by the threatenings of those who sought his downfall, he turned, in his time of trouble, to God in an attitude of praise. "I call to the LORD, who is worthy of praise, and I am saved from my enemies." What a word is this! The way of praise was, for David, the way of deliverance from his problems. Realizing the power of his Creator, David turned from meditating on his problem to praising the Lord, and instantly God's power went to work for him. He knew it could not fail, for he had seen it work time and time again. Praise released God's power into a difficult and dangerous situation.

Turn from your problem right now and focus on God. With all the sincerity of which you are capable, begin to praise Him. Tell Him how great and wonderful He is and how glad you are that He is on your side and you on His. Make much of Jesus in your praise, for God delights in His Son. If the devil tells you that this is manipulation, tell him you will praise God whether He delivers you or not. But mark my words— deliverance will come. The God of David is just the same today.

Lord, thank You for making this day a day of deliverance for me. As I praise You now, I know I shall step out from the dungeon of despair into the sunshine of a bright and glorious victory. Thank You, Father. Amen.

Make much of Jesus in your praise, for God delights in the praise of His Son.

SENDING PRAISE
AHEAD

For Reading and Meditation: Mark 6:30–44

"Jesus took the five loaves and the two fish . . .
and gave thanks" (v. 41 GNB).

Today we look at an incident in the life of Jesus to see how He used praise as the precursor to a miracle. Here in the passage before us, Jesus is presented with a pressing problem. There are thousands of people who have been listening to Him for some time who are now hungry. What should He do? Should He send them away, as the disciples suggested, into the surrounding villages in order to buy food? Jesus is quite clear, however, as to how God wants Him to proceed.

Jesus and Prayer

The interesting thing about the life of Jesus is that whenever He is confronted by a difficult and desperate situation, He always seems to have anticipated it in prayer. Prior to choosing His disciples, He spent some time in prayer (Luke 6:12–13). If you cast your eye back to verse 31 of today's chapter, you will see that Jesus had taken His disciples to a quiet place for a spiritual retreat. Did He do this to prepare them, and Himself, for the miraculous feeding of the five thousand? It would appear so. I have no doubt myself that Jesus used prayer to commune with God and find out what God wanted Him to do in every situation. Then, having sought God's will, He could approach the situation with confident faith and praise.

How did the miracle occur? Did Jesus plead with God for a supernatural display of His power? No, He looked up to heaven, gave thanks, and the bread extended itself in response to His "mighty multiplying touch." It is always right to use prayer as a means of getting to know God's mind on a situation. Then once assured of this, we can send praise and thanksgiving ahead in order to bring back the answer.

> Father, I see that both prayer and praise are important. Help me not to give up one for the sake of the other. Guide me in a right and balanced use. For Jesus' sake. Amen.

Whenever Jesus was confronted with a difficult situation, He always seemed to have anticipated it in prayer.

SINGING JAILBIRDS!

For Reading and Meditation: Acts 16:16–34

"And at midnight Paul and Silas prayed,
and sang praises unto God" (v. 25 KJV).

We are meditating on some biblical instances where praise was used to release God's power into a dark and difficult situation and turn defeat into victory. Today we study the story of Paul and Silas while in prison at Philippi.

Paul and Silas in Prison

After being accused of corrupting the city, Paul and Silas were stripped and beaten until the blood flowed from their bare backs. They were then put in an inner part of the prison and their feet securely clamped in stocks. Paul and Silas refused to believe, however, that God had deserted them or that He was unmindful of their plight. They had a strong inner conviction that everything was working out for God's glory and their good. In such moments it is not necessarily prayer that is needed but praise. As they sat there in the dark dungeon, with the dried blood on their backs and unable to stretch their aching legs, they began to sing hymns of praise to God.

Suddenly, at midnight, there was a great earthquake, the prison doors flew open, and the chains fell off every prisoner. The jailer was horrified. Thinking that he would be held responsible for the situation, he tried to kill himself. Paul, however, shouted to him that all the prisoners were still in the prison and had not escaped. The jailer, sensing that a miracle had occurred, came to Paul and Silas, and said, "Sirs, what must I do to be saved?"

What would have happened, I wonder, if Paul and Silas had sat in the stocks bemoaning their fate? I doubt if a miracle would have taken place. Praise, however, became the note around which God constructed a symphony of sound that broke through the natural barriers to bring freedom and deliverance to His rejoicing children.

Lord, I see that unutterable peace possesses
the hearts of Your children when they have
the right attitudes and do the right things.
Then the consequences are mighty—because they
are in Your hands. I am so thankful. Amen.

Praise turns defeat into victory.

TRY PRAISE

For Reading and Meditation: Psalm 56:1–13

"What time I am afraid,
I will trust in thee" (vv. 3–4 KJV).

Over the past few days we have examined some scriptural examples of where praise was the precursor to a miracle. If we step outside the Scriptures for a moment and examine the writings of some of the great saints of God, we find an almost unanimous agreement that praise is as powerful as prayer in bringing about spiritual victories.

The Great Saints of God

William Law, a great thinker and a great Christian of the eighteenth century, said, "One dark night as I wrestled before God in prayer, I could find no answer. Then I turned to praise. Instantly, the tide turned and I was borne on the wave of a miracle that astonished me and all my household.

Christmas Evans, the Welsh revivalist, said that once when preaching in a church, he found it as "hard as brass." He stopped preaching and began to praise God. "Instantly," he said, "the hardness turned to a wave of spiritual revival. People ran to the front to commit their lives to God. I have never seen a meeting so suddenly transformed."

One dark period, many years ago, I suffered a few weeks of depression that brought me to the verge of giving up the ministry. I tried praying, but the more I prayed the more depressed I felt. The Spirit said, "Try praise." However, I rationalized the issue and persuaded myself that what I was hearing was a voice from my own subconscious. Again the Spirit said, "Try praise." I did, and the heaviness lifted from me within seconds. I felt as if a great weight had been taken off my shoulders. Joy flooded into my heart in response to my praise. From that day to this, serious depression has never once entered my life.

O God, something is opening up before me that I can only feebly understand, yet it beckons me toward new horizons. Help me to put into practice the truth of what You have been teaching me during the last few days. For Jesus' sake. Amen.

Praise is as powerful as prayer in bringing about spiritual victories.

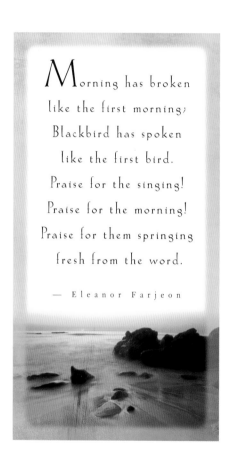

Morning has broken
like the first morning;
Blackbird has spoken
like the first bird.
Praise for the singing!
Praise for the morning!
Praise for them springing
fresh from the word.

— Eleanor Farjeon

REQUIREMENTS FOR THANKFUL WORSHIPERS

God makes space for us in
the covenant family. We are
embraced as children. We belong.
We respond by making space for
God, by being open to God in
our lives, by living thankfully.

— Don Postema

W E E K **DAY 1** F O U R

AN OBEDIENT
HEART

For Reading and Meditation: Matthew 12:30–37

"Out of the overflow of the heart
the mouth speaks" (v. 34).

We have been finding convincing biblical evidence that
praise releases God's power into certain situations and that
heartfelt gratitude to God is often the prelude to a miracle.

Now I intend to bring into the picture several other
considerations. Unless we do so, we are in danger of taking this
truth entirely out of context and of seeing it as the only answer
to all our problems. Every biblical truth suffers from two
great dangers—overemphasis and underemphasis.

One of the books that took the Christian world by storm
two decades ago was *Prison to Praise* by Merlin R. Carothers.
Many Christians, coming from church backgrounds where
praise was rarely mentioned or practiced, overreacted to this
book and came to view praise as the only answer to all their
problems. They overlooked the fact that there were other
spiritual considerations that demanded attention, such as
prayer, Bible reading, and so on.

A Thankful Worshiper

God's Word spells out a number of conditions and requirements for a thankful worshiper, the first of which is an obedient heart. God considers obedience to His Word more important than extravagant sacrifice. An Old Testament prophet, speaking on behalf of the Almighty, said, "To obey is better than sacrifice, and to heed is better than the fat of rams" (1 Sam. 15:22). Since "out of the overflow of the heart the mouth speaks," what we say or sing should reflect the commitment of our hearts to God. If it doesn't, then our efforts to praise, whether it be by vociferous praise or spectacular music, will fail to reach the ears of our Creator God.

O God, help me not to fasten on one truth
to the exclusion of others. I want to be
a balanced Christian—not a biased one.
For Jesus' sake. Amen.

God considers obedience to His Word more important than extravagant sacrifice.

L O S T O N

T H E W A Y U P

For Reading and Meditation: Amos 5:21–24

"Away with the noise of your songs! I will not
listen to the music of your harps" (v. 23).

We said yesterday that God's Word spells out several
conditions required of a thankful worshiper, the first of which
is an obedient heart. If praise does not come from an obedient
heart, it will fail to reach the ears of the Almighty.

A Dream

A minister in a very fashionable church had a dream one
night in which he saw himself standing by the throne of God
in heaven. As he looked down to earth, he saw his congregation
and the one-hundred-voice choir at Sunday worship. The
strange thing was, however, that although he saw the lips of
the choir and the congregation move in song, the only sound
that rose to heaven was that of one solitary voice.

He turned to the Lord and asked for an explanation:
"Why is it, Lord, that out of a congregation of many hundreds

and a choir of a hundred highly trained voices I can hear only a single voice?"

The Lord replied, "The only sound that reaches up to heaven is the sound of heartfelt praise—anything less than this is lost on the way up."

Closer inspection by the minister revealed that the solitary voice reaching heaven was that of a little boy, not even in the choir, who sang the praises of God with utter delight and sincerity.

In Mark 7:6–7, Jesus quotes the prophet Isaiah, "These people honor me with their lips, but their hearts are far from me." Whether our praise is spontaneous or, as with a choir or a singing group, carefully rehearsed and prepared, our sacrifices of thanksgiving and praise must meet God's conditions if they are to be pleasing and acceptable to Him.

O God, enable me to have an obedient heart
so that the expression of thankfulness and
praise is not lost on the way up to heaven.
In Jesus' Name. Amen.

The only sound that reaches up to heaven is the sound of heartfelt praise.

BROKEN

RELATIONSHIPS

For Reading and Meditation: Matthew 5:21–26

"First go and be reconciled to your brother;
then come and offer your gift" (v. 24).

We are seeing that praise and thanksgiving must meet God's conditions if they are to bring joy and pleasure to the Almighty. Today we examine another requirement for a thankful worshiper—reconciliation with fellow Christians.

In today's passage, Jesus shows the order of priority in Christian worship. He is saying in effect: "It's no good coming to God with a sacrifice if you have a broken relationship with a fellow believer. Put that right first and then God will be delighted to accept your offering." We may have the most wonderful sermon to preach, the most delightful music to perform, the most inspiring testimony to give, the most heartfelt praise to present, but if we fail to take the steps necessary to bring about the healing of a broken relationship, then our attempts at worship will never rise higher than the ceiling of the church.

Nests of Hate

In Wales many years ago I knew two ministers, one a Calvinist, the other an Arminian (Calvinism and Arminianism are different theological doctrines). Every Sunday they would denounce each other from their pulpits. As a result, their churches became nests of hate. A Christian leader visited the town and heard of the problem. He invited the men to where he was staying in order, as he said, "to bury the hatchet." They buried the hatchet but left the handle sticking out, so when the leader left town they were at it again.

When the two men eventually put things right between them, stopped denouncing each other, and spoke of each other with love and respect, a spiritual awakening occurred in that town which resulted in some of the greatest songs of praise I have ever heard.

O God, I see so clearly that to try and offer You praise when my heart is full of bitterness or hatred toward another Christian is to dishonor You. This very day help me to heal any broken relationships I have. In Jesus' Name. Amen.

Praise and thanksgiving must meet God's conditions if they are to bring joy and pleasure to the Almighty.

H U M I L I T Y

For Reading and Meditation: Amos 4:1–9

"Bring your sacrifices . . . and brag about your
freewill offerings . . . this is what you love to do"
(vv. 4–5).

Today we examine another of the conditions required of a
true worshiper—genuine humility. A spirit of pride and
self-righteousness can make our sacrifices and thanksgiving
unacceptable, as today's text makes clear. Listen to how it
sounds in the Living Bible: "Go ahead and sacrifice to idols . . .
Keep disobeying—your sins are mounting up. Sacrifice each
morning and bring your tithes twice a week! . . . How you
pride yourselves and crow about it everywhere!"

Spiritual Pride

In fact, an attitude of pride can turn a sacrificial offering of
praise into an act which is sinful. Remember the story of the
Pharisee who gave thanks to God that he was not like the tax
collector? (Luke 18:9–14). It was thanks that was not really
thanks at all. One of the greatest dangers we face as we grow in
our Christian life is the danger of spiritual pride. I have seen
young men leave Bible college, young men with a brilliant

ministry ahead of them, yet I have seen them come crashing down, reduced to nothing because of spiritual pride.

Several weeks ago, after a severe storm, I looked out of my window and saw the branch of a tree lying in the road. A neighbor appeared at that moment and took it away. Later, when I spoke to him about it, he said that parasites had eaten into the branch, weakening it to such an extent that when the storm came, it broke and fell.

"Pride kills thanksgiving," said Henry Ward Beecher, "but a humble mind is the soil out of which thanksgiving naturally grows. A proud man is seldom a grateful man for he never thinks he gets as much as he deserves." The most dangerous parasite I know is spiritual pride. Many are weakened by it and fall in the time of testing.

O God, deliver me from the stranglehold that pride has upon my life, for pride destroys me but humility develops me. For Jesus' sake. Amen.

Thanksgiving naturally grows out of a humble mind.

A REJOICING SPIRIT

For Reading and Meditation: 2 Corinthians 9:6–15;
Exodus 35:29

"For God loves a cheerful giver" (2 Cor. 9:7).

Today we examine yet another condition of a thankful worshiper—a rejoicing spirit. In the passage before us today, Paul tells us that we must give "not reluctantly or under compulsion, for God loves a cheerful giver." Paul, of course, is talking about the giving of money to the work and service of the Lord, but the same principle applies equally to the giving of praise. God loves a cheerful giver. Praise that is not given cheerfully falls short of the ideal.

If expressing your praise is a struggle, something is seriously wrong. If a friend says to you, "I have had a problem with a hasty temper for some time, but I have agonized and struggled over it and now I have found victory," you would probably say, "Splendid, I'm delighted to hear it." If, however, the same friend said to you, "You have done quite a lot for me and I have come to appreciate it, but it has cost me a lot of weary effort," you would probably tell him to keep his appreciation to himself. True thankfulness is spontaneous and happy—or else it falls short of the mark.

The Unwanted Christmas Present

Remember that unwanted Christmas present? When it was given to you, you groped for words of appreciation that wouldn't come. It was kind of the person to give it to you, of course, and you felt you ought to be grateful. You stammered a little. "Thanks," you said, "thanks very much," but deep down inside, you knew it was not real appreciation. However, what happened when you were given something you really wanted? How the words of gratitude tumbled out! "Thanks ever so much. It's just what I wanted." No feeling that you ought to be grateful. You were just grateful—you could not help yourself.

O God, how I long for my gratitude to You to be like that—the spontaneous overflow of a swelling heart. Help me to be a truly grateful person, and not engineer gratitude but give the real thing. Amen.

Praise that is not given cheerfully falls short of the ideal.

" W I T H   G R A C E "

For Reading and Meditation: Colossians 3:16–17;
Ephesians 5:18–20

"Singing with grace in your hearts to the Lord"
(Col. 3:16 KJV).

We continue examining the requirements for a thankful worshiper. Today we look at another quality that is needed to accompany praise given to God—divine grace.

Giving Thanks

The most frequently used word in the New Testament for giving thanks is the Greek word *eucharistein*, which implies intimacy with the person to whom the thanks is given. Matthew uses this word when he records the story of Christ giving thanks to His Father at the Last Supper (Matt. 26:27). The root word for thanksgiving is *charis*, "grace." This is why when giving thanks before a meal we refer to it as "saying grace." However, what does Paul mean when he says that we should praise God "with grace in our hearts to the Lord"?

There are many definitions of grace—all of them inadequate. St. Augustine said, "What is grace? I know until you ask me; when you ask me, I do not know." Grace is goodwill, magnanimity, and bigheartedness. A Christian who has grace will have a generous disposition, will hold no bitterness and harbor no resentment.

I heard of a family who were meticulous in saying grace before meals, but as soon as the meal began they quarreled with each other consistently. One of the children spent a few days with another family who did not only say grace before their meals but demonstrated grace while they ate. There was no bickering, no quarreling. "Now I see why I didn't have an appetite," said the girl. "My family is always quarreling, but since I've been here my appetite has come back. I'm eating normally. I feel well."

You can't praise God genuinely if you have a bitter and quarrelsome spirit. If you do, then you are praising God without grace in your heart.

Lord, I see the folly of trying to praise You
and be at peace with You when my heart is not at
peace with others. Make me a truly gracious person
in everything I do and with everyone I meet.
Then my praise will reach the highest heights
of heaven. Amen.

You can't praise God genuinely if you have a bitter spirit.

F A I T H

For Reading and Meditation: Hebrews 11:1–10

"Without faith it is impossible to please God" (v. 6).

We look at one final condition and requirement for a thankful worshiper—faith. We have been seeing in recent weeks that God commands us to praise Him for everything that happens to us—good, bad, and indifferent (Eph. 5:20). We can only do this when we have the faith and confidence to believe that God is working everything together for the specific good of making us like His Son—conforming us to His image (Rom. 8:28–29).

Kagawa

The condition for enjoying our Christian liberty, says Paul to Timothy, is that we receive everything with thanksgiving (1 Tim. 4:4). I have often referred in my writings to Kagawa, the famous Japanese Christian. He is criticized by many for some of his statements, but even his harshest critics recognized him to be a true man of God.

In his later years, having lost his eyesight, he stubbornly refused to believe that God had finished with him and his life. Faith rose up in him to find a cause for gratitude. He said:

"Having so largely lost my eyesight, the power to see has extended into every part and parcel of my person. Eye blindness means a wider seeing." He went on to say, "I am amazed at the calm that is within me. Every moment I live, I am conscious that I am adventuring with God."

However, the real secret of his faith is revealed in his words, "Despite the lack of my eyesight, the whole creation is mine. God threw it in when He gave me Christ." That is it! All things are ours if we have Christ. As long as I love God and have faith to believe that everything that comes my way can be used for greater effectiveness, then nothing can stop the swelling of praise in my heart. Nothing.

My Father and my God, give me the faith
that locks into Your providence and dares to
believe that good comes out of everything when
You are in it. Amen.

"Despite the lack of my eyesight the whole creation is mine."

Praise releases the power
of God into our lives
and circumstances, because
praise is faith in action.
When we trust God fully,
he is free to work, and he
always brings victory.
It may be a victory that
changes circumstances, or
a victory *in* the circumstances.

— M. R. Carothers

Born To Praise

WEEK 5

FOCUSING ON GOD'S BLESSINGS

Blessings abound
where'er he reigns;
The prisoner leaps to
loose his chains
The weary find eternal rest,
And all the sons
of want are blest.

— Isaac Watts

WORKING WITH
GOD'S DESIGN

For Reading and Meditation: Psalm 103:1–22

"Praise the LORD, O my soul; all my inmost being,
praise his holy name" (v. 1).

Having examined over the past weeks something of the practical benefits of praise, we turn now to consider a question which must be uppermost in many people's minds: What do I do if I don't really feel like praising God? If I give God praise when I don't feel like it, am I not in danger of engineering gratitude? Am I not a hypocrite? The problem is compounded for some when they read in church liturgy such statements as this: "It is very meet, right, and our bounden duty, that we should at all times, and in all places, give thanks unto thee, O Lord." If a person is thankful only because it is "meet, right, and our bounden duty," is that true thankfulness? Thankfulness is like love; it is only truly satisfying when it is spontaneous, when it leaps out of itself, so to speak, when it cannot be held in.

The Wonderful Design

When reading through the psalm I have chosen for today's meditation, you might have said to yourself, "I don't feel like that. The psalmist's sentiments are foreign to me." What then is the way of true thanksgiving?

First we must understand something of the wonderful design of our beings, and work with that design to achieve what God wants and expects of us.

There are three main aspects to our being—will, feelings, and thoughts. Our feelings do not respond to an act of will, but they are greatly influenced by two other factors—right thinking and right behavior. I will be considering both these factors, but let's begin today by determining to fill our thoughts with the right content, for right thinking always produces right feelings.

O Father, help me to feed my thoughts on
the message of Your love and Your goodness.
Then my feelings will carry the message too.
Amen.

Right thinking produces right feelings.

T H I N K !

For Reading and Meditation: Philippians 4:1–8

"If anything is . . . praiseworthy—
think about such things" (v. 8).

We said yesterday that our thoughts greatly affect our feelings. Our emotions follow our thoughts just like baby ducks follow their mother. Although the will is powerless to influence the emotions, this is not true of the thoughts. Thoughts can direct and focus the emotions in a way that can bring about great changes in our feelings. This, then, is the first step on the path of thanksgiving—to think on God's goodness, to fill the mind with the facts concerning His love, and to hold them in the thoughts until they, in turn, have their effect on the emotions.

There is a hymn which says, "Count your blessings"— good but impossible advice? Well, think again—your arithmetic is not good enough! There are a million things of which you are not even aware, but you can think of some of them. So begin to think now. Think of the blessings of the fruitful earth. We draw such wonderful things from it by our toil and sweat, but the sweat and the toil would, in themselves, be useless apart from the blessing of God.

Blessings Worth Thinking About

The great majority of us have never been desperately hungry. While millions of people starve, there is usually enough on our tables. Think about that! Think too of the blessings of love and friendship. If you fell sick, there would no doubt be a loving hand to smooth your pillow. If you suffered bereavement, someone would share your suffering. Love and friendship! Do you have them? They are blessings worth thinking about. Think also of the things which we take so often for granted—the smile of a friend, a birthday or an anniversary, the loyalty of one's family, good health, and so on.

Think, therefore, on God's blessings and be thankful.

O God, forgive me that I am such an ungrateful creature. Help me to focus my thoughts on the abundance of Your blessings so that, in turn, my heart might be full of praise. Amen.

Think on God's blessings and be thankful.

NO REASON FOR THANKSGIVING?

For Reading and Meditation: 2 Corinthians 4: 1–15

"So that the grace that is reaching more
and more people may cause thanksgiving to
overflow to the glory of God" (v. 15).

In 1930 when America was fighting the grip of economic depression, the American Association for the Advancement of Atheism raised a strong protest against the keeping of the annual Thanksgiving Day, which is commemorated on the third Thursday in November. They claimed that in a country where thousands were without jobs, there could be no reason for thanksgiving. Millions, however, ignored their protest and gathered in their homes as usual to give praise and gratitude to God for His blessing upon their lives. How sad that phrase sounds to the ear: "No reason for thanksgiving."

Blessings

No reason for thanksgiving? What of the mercy that lovingly chastens us in our pride and pleasure or the difficulties that drive us to the precipice of human extremity and then push us humbled and penitent into the arms of a loving heavenly Father? And what too of the blessings that come from our Savior Himself—salvation, sanctification, revelation, or the love that overshadows us, encompasses us, and undergirds us?

No reason for thanksgiving? Away with the suggestion! We thank God for the air we breathe, the light by which we see, the kiss of devotion upon the lips of a mother or wife, the cry of a newborn baby, the smell of newly mowed grass. Let us in this disturbed, confused, turbulent, and God-denying generation meditate on the goodness of our God until we build inside our souls a steeple of praise, and install within it the symphonic sounds of everlasting rejoicing.

O God, again I have to confess that I am prone
to see only the shade when the sunshine of
Your love beams all around me. Today, and every
day, with Your help I shall focus more on
the sunshine than the shade. Amen.

In this God-denying generation, meditate on the goodness of God.

A JOURNAL OF GRATEFULNESS

For Reading and Meditation: Philippians 1:3–11

"I thank my God every time I remember you" (v. 3).

If the first step on the pathway to praise is to think about our blessings—and to think on them long and hard—then it makes sense to record the more special blessings in a permanent form, otherwise they might be forgotten.

A missionary, who recorded all his prayer requests, claimed that between 87 and 90 percent of his prayers were answered precisely the way he had asked. Whenever he felt a little discouraged, he would take out his notebook, meditate on the goodness of God to him, and it would not be long, he said, before praise would "bubble up in his soul." Make a practice of noting God's special blessings and, as the hymn I referred to earlier says, "Count your blessings, name them one by one, And it will surprise you what the Lord hath done."

Channels of Blessing

Make a practice, too, of thanking those through whom some of God's blessings come. It does people good to be thanked.

One man I know keeps a Journal of Gratefulness in which he records the names of those whom God has used to encourage or minister to him. Everyone gets a letter of thanks. He got the idea from reading about a well-known writer who had suffered a nervous breakdown and was confined to a hospital room. A friend said to him, "Why don't you list the people who have helped you in your life and write them a letter of thanks?" He did, and this not only turned out to be the basis of his healing but also opened a whole new dimension to his life. He recalled a schoolteacher who had given extra time to teach him, and he wrote to her. She replied, "When I got your letter I was blinded with tears. I taught in school for fifty years, and yours is the first note of appreciation I have ever received. I shall cherish it until the day I die."

Father, if there is someone to whom I should say thank you, help me to recall the situation and make contact with them—for Your own dear Name's sake. Amen.

Record special blessings; otherwise they might be forgotten.

THANKSGIVING
FOR EVERYTHING

For Reading and Meditation: 1 Thessalonians 5:16–24

"Give thanks in all circumstances, for this
is God's will for you in Christ Jesus" (v. 18).

We continue today considering the importance of a
personal "thank you" not only to God but also to those who
have helped us or ministered to us. "Pride," says one writer,
"is believing that I achieved what in reality God and others
did for me and through me."

Just One Letter

Think back as far as you can remember to all the people
who have benefited your life. Have you ever thanked them?
Eventually you might want to thank them all, but begin by
selecting one and send him or her a letter of appreciation.
The way to accomplish a seemingly impossible task is to break
it down into achievable goals. Your first goal should be just
one letter.

One man I knew wrote not only to his former schoolteacher
but also to a bishop who had been of great spiritual help to him.

Although the thanks was belated, this is what the bishop said in reply: "Your letter was so beautiful, so real, that as I sat reading it in my study, the tears fell from my eyes—tears of gratitude. My wife is now dead, but before I realized what I was doing I rose from my chair and called her name to show it to her, forgetting for a moment that she was gone. You will never know how much your letter has warmed my spirit. I have been walking about in the glow of it all day long."

Need I say anything more? So make a practice of thanking people. It will please God. He often sends His special mercies by the hands of other people, and He likes His messengers to be thanked also. Gratitude is only as sincere as the effort you make to express it. "Someone, somewhere is waiting for a letter from you."

Lord, don't let me wriggle past this challenge
or try to rationalize it in anyway.
Make me a thankful person—to both You
and Your messengers. Amen.

Gratitude is only as sincere as the effort you make to express it.

A RANSOMED SINNER

For Reading and Meditation: 2 Corinthians 9:6–15

"Thank God for his Son—his Gift
too wonderful for words" (v. 15 TLB).

We continue meditating on the importance of focusing our thoughts on God's blessings in our lives so that right thinking can produce the right feelings. What is the greatest blessing God has given us? There can be no doubt about that—it is Christ! The blessing of knowing Him is so great that as Paul says in the text before us today, it's just "too wonderful for words."

Baron Von Huegel

Have you ever thought what your life would be like without Jesus Christ? It would be a dark picture. When Baron Von Huegel considered that question, he said, "I should be . . . a corrupt, or at least an incredibly unhappy, violent, bitter, self-occupied, self-destructive soul, were it not for Christ and for Him having come and saved me from myself." You and I might phrase it differently, but we would all share the same conclusion: Without Christ we would be utterly self-centered and self-engrossed.

I met Christ fifty years ago at the front of a church in South Wales. I came to Him with nothing to offer except my moral and spiritual bankruptcy. To my amazement He took me, forgave me, reconciled me to God, to myself, to others, to nature, to life, and sent my soul singing its way down through the years.

A missionary traveling on a plane was given a card with his meal. On it was written: "What do you think of our meals?" He wrote: "Too good for a ransomed sinner." When the stewardess read the card, she smiled and asked him what he meant. He told her that this was the way he looked at everything—not just a meal. He saw everything in the light of being a ransomed sinner. How do you take things—for granted or with gratitude?

> Blessed Savior, I wonder if I will ever get
> over the wonder of being a ransomed sinner?
> I doubt it, nor do I want to get over it.
> I shall be grateful for all eternity. Amen.

How do you take things—for granted or with gratitude?

ACHIEVING
THE IMPOSSIBLE

For Reading and Meditation: Philippians 2:12–18

"God is at work within you, helping you
want to obey him, and then helping you do
what he wants" (v. 13 TLB).

We have been studying for the past few days the importance
of thinking about God's multiplied mercies in order to prime
the pump of praise in our hearts. We cannot by an act of will
change our feelings, but we can use our will to focus on right
thoughts, and these, in turn, bring about right feelings. God
doesn't hold us responsible for our feelings, but He does
hold us responsible for what we do with our wills.

The Will

The will can be used in another direction also—to bring
about changes in the way we act and behave. Stanley Jones said,
"It is easier to act yourself into a new way of thinking than
to think yourself into a new way of acting." Now don't
misunderstand this. He is not saying it is better but easier.
The focusing of thoughts may be difficult for some people,

especially if you are down in the dumps or depressed. If this is a problem and you can't use your will to focus your thoughts on God's blessings, then use your will to change your behavior.

Act of Faith

I once asked a depressed person to read aloud Psalm 136. He did—dolefully. "Now read it again," I said, "but this time throw back your shoulders, say the words with emphasis, and imagine how you would say it if you really believed what you are reading." He did what I asked and said that immediately he felt better. I got him to read it several times in this way and his depression lifted. (Not all depression, of course, responds to this method.) There is an important principle here. When we use our wills to do what God asks us to do—praise Him even though we don't feel like it—He responds to this act of faith by bringing about a change in our feelings—miraculously.

O Father, help me to understand and apply
this important principle to my personality.
Give me the faith that believes that when I do
the possible, You will do the impossible. Amen.

The will can bring about changes in the way we act and behave.

The God of
Abraham praise who
reigns enthroned above,
ancient of everlasting days,
and God of Love;
Jehovah, great I am by
earth and heaven confessed!
I bow and bless the sacred
name for ever blest.

— Thomas Olivers

Journal Entry

WEEK 6

RESPONDING TO LIFE'S DIFFICULTIES

O worship the King,
all-glorious above;
O gratefully sing his power
and his love;
Our Shield and Defender,
the Ancient of Days,
Pavilioned in splendour,
and girded with praise.

— Sir Robert Grant

THE ONE
CENTRAL TRUTH

For Reading and Meditation: 2 Corinthians 2:1–17

"But thanks be to God, who in Christ always
leads us in triumph" (v. 14 RSV).

We saw last week that what holds our thoughts holds our emotions. It follows, therefore, that if we work on the content of our thoughts, this, in turn, will determine the content of our emotions. This week we shall examine one of the most vital truths a Christian must grasp if his life is to be free from strain and become a paean of praise.

A letter I received contained this request: "Is there a central truth, one dominant unifying concept which a Christian must believe, which, more than anything else, enables him to face all the adversities and discouragements of life triumphantly?" I replied that there was, and I gave what in my view is the most sustaining truth of the Christian life: It is not so much what happens to us that is important but how we respond to it. We are what we respond to—nothing more and nothing less.

Reacting to Problems

Toynbee, the great historian, said, "When a civilization—or an individual—comes up against a problem, it or he will react in one of four ways: (a) archaism, (b) futurism, (c) detachment, (d) transformation." The first three represent a fleeing from the issue, the fourth, a facing of the issue, and transforming it into something better. When we hit a problem, we will probably adopt one of these four attitudes in order to find a solution. We will retreat into the past, escape into the future, withdraw in inner detachment, or take everything that comes—good, bad, and indifferent—and turn it into something else. Only a Christian can take the last of these ways, as only the Christian faith has the power to turn every difficulty into a discovery, every test into a triumph, every setback into a springboard.

My Father and my God, I sense today that
I am on the verge of discovering the secret of poise
and power in the Christian life. Hold me steady
so that I shall not miss one single aspect of it.
In Jesus' Name I pray. Amen.

Only the Christian faith provides the power to turn every difficulty into a discovery.

W E E K **DAY 2** S I X

THE WAY OF TRANSFORMATION

For Reading and Meditation: Psalm 139:7–12

"Even there your hand will guide me,
your strength will support me" (v. 10 TLB).

There are various ways in which we can respond to life's difficulties and problems, but the Christian way is the way of transformation. By transformation I mean the facing of life as it comes, day by day, and transforming the bad things that come into something positive and beneficial. If you adopt this attitude to life and make it a central conviction, you will inevitably become a truly praising person.

Mental Illness

A famous psychiatrist said, "Thankfulness is the perfect antidote for mental illness." But what is mental illness? I took a book on the subject of psychology off my bookshelf to find out. This is what it said, "Mental illness is a fear of reality— a lack of awareness, an escape from the present." This is a limited definition, of course, but it is a fact that the mentally ill find it difficult to face reality while the mentally healthy are better equipped to face life with calmness and confidence.

But what is reality? Reality is seeing life as it is. Life comes to us with many problems—injustice, deceit, pain, hurt, the disloyalty of friends, sickness, accidents, disease, and so on. For the Christian, however, there is another side to this. Reality includes the sovereignty of God, the loving purposes of the Almighty, and the providential care that He has for His own. If a Christian doesn't see the full perspective—that God is in control of the universe and that He is at work turning every stumbling block into a stepping-stone—it is quite possible that he will succumb to difficult situations, because he is failing to respond correctly.

Reality, for the Christian, is bringing Jesus alongside all of life's problems and seeing life from His point of view.

O God, I am so thankful that I don't need to run away from anything. I can meet everything with a song—a song of victory. Transformation is my open door into reality. Amen.

God is at work turning every stumbling block into a stepping-stone.

MAKE
EVERYTHING SERVE

For Reading and Meditation: 2 Corinthians 4:7–18

"We are hard pressed . . . but not crushed . . .
struck down, but not destroyed" (vv. 8–9).

Today we ask ourselves, How did Jesus face difficulties
and problems in His own life? Did He retreat into the past,
escape into the future, withdraw into Himself, or take
everything that came and transform it?

The Way of Transformation

Jesus actually took the same way of transformation.
He refused to retreat into Israel's glorious past, refused to escape
into the glorious future of the kingdom of God, refused to
withdraw in detachment as did the Pharisees (the separatists).
He faced life realistically and made it serve Him.

He was employed as a carpenter, and as He worked He
made Himself ready for the day when He would build a new
humanity. He met temptation in the wilderness and made it
serve Him and strengthen Him. He went into the wilderness
"full of the Holy Spirit" and came out "in the power of the

Spirit" (Luke 4:1, 14). Temptation turned fullness into power. He took twelve ordinary men and made them into preachers and teachers who changed the course of history. He sat by a well in a little town called Sychar, in the despised province of Samaria, and led a woman into salvation, whereupon she became an evangelist to the whole village, saying, "Come, see a man who told me everything I ever did" (John 4:29).

When He was criticized by the people of His day for eating with publicans and sinners, He took the criticism and transformed it into three parables—the lost sheep, the lost coin, and the lost son (Luke 15). These are without doubt the most beautiful parables ever uttered, showing the heart of a seeking, loving, redemptive God. He took a reviling and turned it into a revelation.

O Father, I see so clearly that if I hold this tremendous truth in my heart—that with You I can transform everything that comes—then praise will be as natural to me as the very air I breathe. Thank You, Father. Amen.

He took a reviling and turned it into a revelation.

A RADIANT PHILOSOPHY

For Reading and Meditation: Hebrews 13:1–8

"For God has said, 'I will never . . . fail you nor forsake you.' That is why we can say . . . 'The Lord is my Helper and I am not afraid of anything'" (vv. 5–6 TLB).

I was once asked, Is there one central truth which a Christian must believe, which, more than anything else, will enable him to face all the adversities of life triumphantly? I replied that there was. It is not so much what happens to us that is important but how we respond to it. This was the truth that filled the content of Jesus' life, and it gave Him a peace and a poise that kept Him unperturbed even in the midst of a storm!

Jesus' Disciples

Was this a characteristic of Jesus only? No, His disciples possessed it too. Acts 5:40–41 tells us that after the apostles had been beaten, they left the presence of the council rejoicing. Rejoicing over injustice! When you can rejoice at an injustice done to you, then you are really triumphant. You have transformed the worst into the best. A joyous Christian was arrested for preaching on the street. He said to one of the policemen who led him away, "If you have the same opinion of me as I have of you, then we are going to have a wonderful time together." The policeman didn't know what to do with the man and let him go! The man transformed the situation with his goodwill.

A New Testament text referring to Joseph says: "And the patriarchs, jealous of Joseph, sold him into Egypt; but God . . ." (Acts 7:9 RSV). That phrase, "But God," is at the end of every injustice and every problem. He has the last word. Christ can transform every bad thing that comes your way—sorrow, pain, hurt, disloyalty, bereavement—everything, providing you let Him. This is an incomparable philosophy of life—and a radiant one.

Lord Jesus, with this secret in my heart, I can face everything in the knowledge that life can do nothing to me, and I can do everything to it—I can transform it. Praise Your wonderful Name. Amen.

When you can rejoice at an injustice done to you, then you are really triumphant.

REDEMPTIVE
REACTIONS

For Reading and Meditation: Luke 10:25–37

"On one occasion an expert in the law
stood up to test Jesus" (v. 25).

The issue of developing right responses to what happens to us deserves some further meditation. A modern writer says, "Religion is occupied to a great degree with the performance of right actions—do this, don't do that and so on." This is important, but it is only half the truth.

Right Reactions

Right actions are an essential and integral part of the Christian message, but so are right reactions. Some people would go so far as to say that our reactions are more important than our actions. There are many people who do not lie, cheat, steal, or commit adultery. They are outwardly correct in their actions, but they may be upset and inwardly disrupted by wrong reactions to what life and other people do to them. Drunkenness, adultery, lying, cheating, and stealing can cloud the countenance and make the lines of the face sag. However, just as definitely will the same thing happen to you if you react to life with self-pity, resentment, fear, jealousy, or retaliation. These and other negative reactions make for a disrupted interior and a sad face.

The actions of Jesus were wonderful, but so were His reactions. About half the Gospels are taken up with a description of His actions and the other half with His reactions. And His reactions were as redemptive and revealing as His actions. When a lawyer stood up to put Him to the test, He answered his question and then gave the world the unforgettable story of the Good Samaritan. On the cross, He prayed, "Father, forgive them, for they do not know what they are doing" (Luke 23:34). The highest reaction to the greatest injustice. That reaction revealed the nature of God as redemptive love in final terms.

Lord Jesus, how can I thank You enough
for showing me how to react to life.
Now I have the key; help me to place it in
the locked doors I face today and react
redemptively to everything. Amen.

Jesus' reactions were as redemptive and revealing as His actions.

TURNING HELL INTO HEAVEN

For Reading and Meditation: 1 Corinthians 13:1–13

"Love never fails" (v. 8).

We are seeing that there is a Christian way to react to everything that comes, and right reactions are just as important as right actions.

God's Grace

Some years ago a woman sought the advice of a Christian counselor on whether she should get a divorce. After hearing her story, the counselor said, "If what you have said is true, then if ever a woman had a right to a divorce, you have one." The husband had broken every moral law and brutalized his wife so much that she had to spend nights away from home in fear for her physical safety. The counselor went on to say, however, "The question is not so much what is your right, but whether you can take the grace of God in this situation and let it make you better."

I know many Christian counselors who would refrain from giving that kind of advice, but this one felt it was what God would have him say. The woman refrained from instituting divorce proceedings and went through another five years of hell—literally. Her husband would lock her out of the house in drunken fits, even nailing up the doors. He destroyed some of her clothes and smeared the rest with boot polish. She prayed every day, "Lord, teach me how to respond to this situation so that I might make it serve the ends of Your kingdom."

She continued to show such love to her husband that eventually her love broke him. He gave his life to Christ, stopped drinking, and rebuilt his business. The daughter told her mother, "If that had been me, I doubt whether I could have done it." But the mother, by utilizing the grace God gave her and reacting in a loving way, succeeded in turning a hell into a heaven.

Father, I wonder how I would have responded in this situation. One thing is clear—there is a great gap between what I am and what I know I can be. Help me to close that gap—beginning today. For Jesus' sake. Amen.

"Lord, make this problem serve the ends of Your kingdom."

U N R E S O L V E D
C O N F L I C T S

For Reading and Meditation: Luke 9:51–56

"When the disciples . . . saw this, they asked,
'Lord, do you want us to call fire down from heaven
to destroy them?'" (v. 54).

We continue meditating on the need for developing right reactions to life. In this world a Christian is bound to be treated unchristianly, for humanity is largely unchristian. The reactions to unchristian treatment become as important as our actions.

I knew a woman who, because her family was treating her badly, developed a good deal of self-pity which pushed her toward a martyr complex. One day someone gave her a copy of *Every Day with Jesus* on "How to be Stable in an Unstable World." Through it, she saw how much she was drifting from the Christian position and surrendered her attitude of self-pity. She wrote to me to say, "If that book had not fallen into my hands at that time, I think I would have drifted too far into a martyrdom complex to have come back."

A Male Nurse

I know another person, a male nurse, who got so drowsy during his duties that he sometimes went to sleep on his feet! His doctor thought it was sleeping sickness, but after a number of tests and examinations he said it was psychosomatic—i.e., triggered by emotional problems. The man contacted a Christian counselor who discovered that beneath the surface of his life was a deep inner conflict. He had been rejected as a missionary some years before, and this had produced a deep inferiority complex. It had also made him very resentful, and the two problems combined resulted in his wanting to get away from life. The sleepiness was an outer symptom of an inner desire to dull the pain and problem of his life. When the inferiority and resentment were surrendered to God, he became a new person—spiritually and physically.

My Father and my God, I know I can only be fully effective when I give up every unchristian reaction. From today, and by Your grace, I shall no longer play nursemaid to any resentment or wrong reaction. Help me, Lord Jesus. Amen.

Reactions to unchristian treatment become as important as our actions.

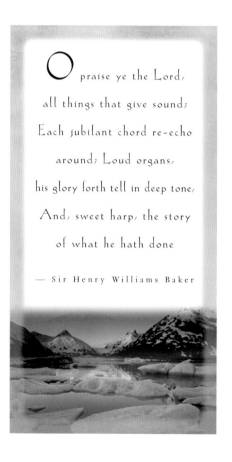

O praise ye the Lord,
all things that give sound;
Each jubilant chord re-echo
around; Loud organs,
his glory forth tell in deep tone,
And, sweet harp, the story
of what he hath done

— Sir Henry Williams Baker

Born To Praise

Journal Entry

Born To Praise

OVERCOMING WRONG REACTIONS

Let us with a gladsome mind

Praise the Lord, for he is kind,

For his mercies ay endure,

Ever faithful, ever sure.

— John Milton

A LADDER TO
RIGHT REACTIONS

For Reading and Meditation: Romans 12:9–21

"Do not be overcome by evil, but overcome evil
with good" (v. 21).

We have seen enough to convince us that if we are to enjoy a life of continued praise, we must pay attention not only to our actions but to our reactions as well. As this matter of right reactions is so important to spiritual and physical health, let me offer you a ladder by which you can climb out of the pit of distorted thinking.

Spend some time quietly before God going over your life to see if you are reacting wrongly to life's situations. God knows all about us because He is omniscient, but the question is, Do we know all there is to know about ourselves? The answer, of course, is that we don't, for there are areas deep within us which respond only to honest self-examination. Psalm 139 begins by stating that God knows everything about us and concludes with the psalmist asking that he might be searched by God. If God knows everything there is to know about us, why pray that He might search us? Because each person needs to know more about himself. Ask God to help you see yourself as He sees you, from within. You have been looking at life from a certain angle, and it will not be easy for you to see yourself differently unless He comes to your aid. You will need divine aid to shift to God's viewpoint.

Be alert to the fact that you will try to defend yourself since defenses have been built up by you over many years to justify your reactions. Many of us argue ourselves into self-justification of our reactions so that it is not easy to admit we are wrong. It is far easier to confess wrong actions than wrong reactions. Pay special attention to this, for unless you win at this point you will be blocked all along the way.

Lord Jesus, I see You are wanting to save me completely from wrong reactions and wrong actions. I consent to what You are doing in my life today, and I surrender both of these to You now. For Your praise and glory. Amen.

It is far easier to confess wrong actions than wrong reactions.

L I K E

P R O D U C E S   L I K E

For Reading and Meditation: Mark 3:20–30

"How can Satan drive out Satan?" (v. 23).

We continue building a ladder to help us overcome wrong reactions. Before we go on to the next step, however, we pause to consider what we said yesterday. It is easier, we said, to confess wrong actions than wrong reactions, for the wrong reactions take place deep within us, away from the glare and scrutiny of the public gaze. Someone has said that "wrong reactions are the vice of the virtuous." Virtuous people can point to wrongs being done to them and use the outer wrongs to justify the inner wrongs. However, there can be no justification for wrong reactions, for whether seemingly justified by the actions of others or not, they are inwardly devastating. To justify them will not take away their evil effects—in you.

Leave No Roots

Be relentless with wrong reactions, uproot them, get them

out, leave no roots to sprout again. It's no good chopping away at the trunk or the branches if the roots are allowed to remain. A man once said to me, when I pleaded with him to give up his resentment of a fellow Christian, "But my resentment of him is keeping him under control; God is using my resentment redemptively. It may be a wrong means, but it will achieve a right end." However, resentment is a false means and will only succeed in bringing a person to a false end. Can Satan drive out Satan? Can you by acting like the devil get the devil out of people? Like produces like. A bitter spring produces a bitter stream, and resentment produces resentment. Dig remorselessly into your life and make sure that everything is brought up and out. A partial surrender ends only in total defeat.

> Lord, I want to take a step once and
> for all away from wrong reactions to right
> reactions. I do it now, in Your presence,
> firmly, positively and conclusively.
> For Your own dear Name's sake. Amen.

A partial surrender ends only in total defeat.

W   E   E   K   **DAY 3**   S   E   V   E   N

BE READY
TO CHANGE

For Reading and Meditation: Philippians 3:1–11

"Whatever was to my profit I now consider loss
for the sake of Christ" (v. 7).

We continue climbing the ladder that leads us out of
wrong reactions.

Resist the built-in desire you have to stay as you are,
and make up your mind that with God's help you are going
to change. There is something about human nature that
resists change. We cling to old habits and desires simply
because, like shoes we have worn for some time, they feel
comfortable and secure. Many of the ceremonies in the
House of Commons in Great Britain are out-of-date and
have no relevance to a modern generation, but the
traditionalists say, "Let things remain as they are—there is
no real need to change." The outdated ceremonies of the
House of Commons harm no one, but there are many things
that we cling to in our lives which must go if we are to
move on into maturity in our Christian lives. We are disturbed
by change. Our ability and willingness to change for the

better into Christlikeness, however, determines our spiritual poise and power.

The Worst Thing

Picture the worst thing that can happen to you, and imagine yourself responding to it with praise. Unless you can be thankful for the worst that can happen, then you are a candidate for insecurity. "No man," said Professor John Joyce, "is safe unless he can stand anything that can happen to him." At the heart of many lives is a worm eating away that says, "Suppose this is taken away or lost or destroyed—what then?" When I say "worst," I have to make one exception—sin. You can't be thankful for that! A Christian, with God's help, can stand anything that happens to him. And why? Because whatever happens to him can be used for greater and higher purposes.

O Father, already I can feel my feet on this ladder to right reactions. In You I am safe, for nothing can work successfully against me. Eternal praise be to Your Name. Amen.

Christians, with God's help, can stand anything that happens to them.

"IT COMES TO PASS"

For Reading and Meditation: Psalm 30:1–12

"Weeping may endure for a night, but joy cometh in the morning" (v. 5 KJV).

We come now to the last two steps on the ladder out of wrong reactions.

God's Forgiveness

Accept God's forgiveness for your wrong reactions as well as for your wrong actions. God is as eager to deliver you from your wrong reactions as from your wrong actions. The father in the story of the Prodigal Son wanted to restore his younger son who had sinned by his actions, but he was just as eager to restore the elder son who had sinned by his wrong reactions of bitterness and unforgiveness. If at the end of the story the younger son was "inside" the family circle and the elder son was "outside," it was not because redemption was not extended to both.

Realize that everything that comes—comes to pass. A preacher with little education was asked what Bible verse he loved most. He replied, "And it came to pass." When pressed for the reason for this strange choice, he replied, "Well, problems and difficulties come our way, but they come to 'pass.'" His application of that particular text was not accurate biblical interpretation, but as someone said who heard him make the remark, "It was unsoundly sound!" Troubles come—but they come to pass.

Our text for today says, "Weeping may endure for a night, but joy cometh in the morning." The sorrow comes and passes, but the joy goes on forever. In the midst of life's difficult problems, say to yourself, "It comes—but it comes to pass." Then take hold of God's grace and remain steady. Are you facing a storm at this very moment? Then I have a word from God for you: hold on to God and ride out the storm. It has come—but it will come to pass.

O God, my Father, I am thankful that my light afflictions, which are but for the moment, are working out for me "a far more exceeding and eternal weight of glory." I can sit still. Help me to do so. Amen.

Take hold of God's grace and remain steady.

THE PTLA CLUB

For Reading and Meditation: Romans 12:9–21

"Rejoice with those who rejoice;
mourn with those who mourn" (v. 15).

As we come to our last few days together, I want to share with you some words of caution and admonition. First, let us be on our guard that we do not reduce praise to the level of mere clichés.

I heard some years ago of a group of Christians who called themselves "The PTLA Club." The initials PTLA, I understand, mean "Praise the Lord Anyway." I have it on good authority that on one occasion the group visited the home of a father and mother whose son had been killed by a hit-and-run driver while walking home from school.

"Well, PTLA," said the spokesman for the group to the grieving parents.

"PTLA?" said the father. "I'm afraid I don't understand what you mean."

"Praise the Lord anyway," said the spokesman. "If you do that, you will stop concentrating on your problem, and you will feel a lot better for it."

Can you think of anything more insensitive than that

remark? There was nothing wrong with the advice to praise the Lord, but in this case it was ill-timed and inappropriate.

Christian Schizophrenia

What is it that makes Christians mouth important statements such as "Praise the Lord" and turn them into clichés? There are many reasons, but the main one is a lack of deep faith in the providence of God, and so they try to reassure themselves with nice-sounding phrases. It is a form of escapism which seeks to dull the harshness of reality. One Christian psychiatrist refers to it as a form of Christian schizophrenia—a faith that maintains itself by means of a fantasy world, completely divorced from the real world of pain, suffering, evil, and a cross.

> O Father, make me sensitive to the hurts
> and suffering of others so that I do not gloss
> over their problems with a quick PTLA.
> I must be careful not only what I say but
> also when I say it. Amen.

Many Christians lack a deep faith in the providence of God.

WE ARE FREE!

For Reading and Meditation: 1 John 4:7–21

*"This is love: not that we loved God,
but that he loved us" (v. 10).*

Another danger to avoid in relation to this matter of praise is seeing it as a means by which we earn God's love. Some Christians regard praise as a good piece of behavior by which they earn God's approval. God does not love us because we are thankful; rather, we are thankful because He loves us.

God Already Loves You

We saw right at the beginning of our studies that God has no needs. He doesn't need our gifts. He doesn't need our sacrifices. He doesn't need our thanks. We are free! God's attitude toward us is the same—love—no matter what our attitude or response to Him may be. Isn't this incredible? It is so bewildering that multitudes of Christians stumble over it, particularly those who spent the early part of their lives trying to get an insensitive parent, or parents, to love them. Let me assure you that all the thankfulness in the world cannot pull one ounce more love out of God than He already gives you. Your thankfulness certainly changes you so that you can receive more of that love, but the block is never in Him—it is in you. Nothing you can do can motivate God to love you more than He does, for He already loves you with all the force and energy of His being.

Because we are free to be thankful, this presents us with a uniquely human possibility—the choice to respond to Him spontaneously in thankfulness. As we have seen over and over again during the past few weeks, genuine thanks is freely given. How could it be genuine if it is conditional or coerced? Let the wonder of this truth sink deep into your soul as I spell it out again. God does not love you because you are thankful—you are thankful because He loves you.

Gracious Father, help me to focus on this truth until the wonder of it drives me forward in more active and fruitful service than I have ever known before. For Jesus' sake. Amen.

God does not love us because we are thankful; rather, we are thankful because He loves us.

Not Enough Stars!

For Reading and Meditation: Psalm 145:1–21

"Great is the LORD, and greatly
to be praised" (v. 3 KJV).

We come now to the last day in our meditations on praise and worship. One consideration remains as we draw to a close—what endless reasons we have to be thankful! We are often rebuked in our thanklessness by people less fortunate than ourselves and, conversely, we are often reminded by them of the number and source of our blessings.

Phelp's Box

A minister told how he used to visit an invalid girl. She was a delightful Christian, but because of her affliction she was confined to a "Phelp's box." It looked like a shallow coffin, and it was used many years ago for children who suffered from curvature of the spine. The little girl of whom the minister spoke was strapped into this box, and here she lived day and night, being taken out only for an hour or two a day. She asked that her box be put near the window so she could see the sky.

One day she said to the minister, "In this position I can only look up, and on those nights when I find it difficult to sleep, I play with the stars."

"How do you play with the stars?" asked the minister.

"Well," she said, "I pick out the brightest star I can find and I say, 'That's Mommy.' I pick out another one and say, 'That's Daddy.' I find a twinkling one for my brother, my puppy, my doctor, my spinal perambulator . . ." On and on she went. Her list seemed endless and some time later, when she seemed to be running out of breath, she said, "But there just aren't enough stars to go around."

If after completing these readings you think you have no reasons to be thankful, then look out tonight and count the stars. There aren't enough stars to go around.

O God, take these meditations on praise
and turn them into a burning glass that sets fire
to my soul. You have given me so much:
give me one thing more—a praising heart.
For Jesus' sake I ask it. Amen.

What endless reasons we have to be thankful!

All people
that on earth do dwell,
Sing to the Lord with
cheerful voice;
Him serve with fear,
his praise forth tell, Come
ye before him, and rejoice.

— William Kethe